Entering the Path

Outer and Inner Refuge

GW00713289

Entering
the Path

Outer and Inner Refuge

by

Dzogchen Ponlop
Rinpoche

SIDDHI PUBLICATIONS
Vancouver, Canada 2000

SIDDHI PUBLICATIONS
P.O. Box 93542
RPO Nelson Park
Vancouver, British Columbia
Canada
V6E 4L7

E-mail:
siddhipubs@nalandabodhi.org

ISBN 0-9687689-3-8

Second edition October 2000

ENTERING THE PATH
Outer and Inner Refuge

Contents

THE REFUGE VOW

Preceptor, please consider me. I, from now throughout the duration of my life, take refuge in the Buddha, the most supreme of human beings;

I take refuge in the Dharma, the most supreme of all that is free of attachment;

I take refuge in the Sangha, the most supreme of assemblies;

Preceptor, please accept me as a Buddhist who will hold the three refuges from now throughout the duration of my life.

ENTERING THE PATH
Outer and Inner Refuge

INTRODUCTION

There are three sources of refuge. The sources to whom one goes for refuge are the Three Jewels. These are the Buddha, Dharma and Sangha. The reason one goes for Refuge to them is that one has recognized samsara as being a situation of suffering and fear. In order to alleviate suffering and fear, and to remove their causes, one goes to the sources of refuge as protectors.

Generally speaking, there are two styles of going for Refuge. There is a style of going for refuge to the Buddha, Dharma, and Sangha in their external forms as something separate from oneself. This is an approach based on relative reality.

There is a second style of refuge based on absolute reality where you go for refuge to the Three Jewels as something internal, as something that is part of your mind. From this point of view, the Buddha, Dharma and Sangha are not far away from you. They are quite close to you. As a matter of fact, they are so close that you can't see them. We are going through both styles as a two-stage process.

OUTER REFUGE

In the initial ceremony, we're principally concerned with the external refuge. We take refuge in the historic Buddha as an example; in the dharma, the teachings of Buddha, as the path; and in the Sangha, the Assembly, as our companion. These are the three outer refuges.

The outer form of refuge is simply a confirmation through our body, speech, and mind of the innermost discovery of refuge. Taking refuge in the outer sense is the process of strengthening and confirming our confidence, our trust, and our basic sense of courage. We take refuge simply within our heart, within our mind. We do this in order to further our understanding and realization of this enlightened heart.

An analogy for this is to imagine ourselves sitting in our room saying,

"I am going to give five dollars to a panhandler tomorrow when I go out on the street." You know, we have that sort of nice, enlightened, compassionate heart. But when we walk outside and see a panhandler, we may instinctively just pass by without making any effort to bring our wallets out of our pockets. It's very simple and easy to just pass by the panhandler the next day. This is like having some sense of inner refuge but not going through with the outer form of refuge.

However, we may pass by a panhandler today and say, "OK, I don't have the money now but I'm going to bring you five dollars tomorrow." You promise that to him and then you go back to your home. The next day, when you go out, it's pretty sure that you will have the five dollars to give to him or her on the street. So, when you go out next day, there's a much stronger commitment involved. You know that you will really give five dollars rather than just think about giving.

Therefore, taking refuge in the outer sense strengthens our heart, our path, and our practice. That is why the outer refuge is so strongly emphasized in entering the path of Buddhadharma.

Taking Refuge in The Buddha

The first object of our refuge is the Buddha Shakyamuni, the historic Buddha. The Buddha protects by teaching. When we take refuge in the Buddha, we're taking refuge in Buddha Shakyamuni and in all of the Buddhas of the past, future and present. When we take this refuge in Buddha as an example, we're not taking refuge in Buddha as a god or as some supernatural being outside of ourselves. We're taking refuge in

Buddha as a basic human being, a supreme human teacher, who achieved the complete state of enlightenment.

We take refuge and pay respect to Buddha Shakyamuni not only because of his attainment of enlightenment but because of his compassionate loving heart and his sharing of his path; the sharing of his enlightenment with all of us. To show our appreciation for his kindness and wisdom, we pay respect. We bow to Buddha.

We take refuge in Buddha Shakyamuni as a simple teacher; a Nirmanakaya Buddha who was a human being. He was a prince of India. He walked on our earth. He ate our food. He went through all the suffering and pain of being human as well as the suffering and pain of not only one dathun (one month of sitting practice), but six years of dathuns. Through this, we have a basic connection with Buddha. We can make a basic connection with Buddha from the pain of dathun sitting.

As a real human being, he went through this path and achieved the final realization of enlightenment. In this way, he is an example for us. He has given us the wisdom and realization of this path without keeping anything for himself. He has given everything to us. Therefore, we take refuge in the Samyak-sambuddha, the perfect Buddha, and in his mind; which is the Dharmakaya. We appreciate his wisdom and kindness.

Out of his great love and great wisdom, Buddha taught methods that can lead one to that same attainment of enlightenment. The attitude of going for refuge in the Buddha as an example is: "If he can do it as a real human being, then I can. Just as he succeeded in actually attaining Buddhahood, through training in the path leading to liberation and omniscience, therefore so will I."

Buddha himself proclaimed in one of his first teachings, referring to the Hindu notion of purifying one's karma by bathing in the River Ganges, that Buddhas cannot purify your karma with water. He said, "I cannot purify your karma by pouring water from a golden vase, a diamond vase, or whatever vase you have. I cannot purify your karma, your negativities, by that means. I cannot give my realization to you by my hand. I cannot transfer my realization. I don't have that power." But he also said, "What Buddhas can do is show the path of liberation, the path of enlightenment. It is totally up to you how you walk on this path, how you handle this path."

From this very verse, we can see that we're not taking refuge in the Buddha as a supernatural being outside ourselves who holds the keyboard to our computer. What Buddha is saying here is that you are holding your own keyboard. What you are learning from him are the command keys.

You are learning the skill of pressing the keys to get the programs that you want to see on the screen. The keys are always in front of us. Whether we press the right key or not is only a question of our knowledge.

What Buddha is teaching us is the path, the way we can attain enlightenment. He is not saving us from samsara. He does not have the power to purify our karma and so forth. We're not taking refuge in Buddha in that sense. We're taking refuge in Buddha in the sense that he is an enlightened teacher who has shown the right path of enlightenment and liberation. He is an example of our capacity or potential. We go to him for refuge in the sense of aspiring to attain exactly that same realization.

That is the Nirmanakaya Buddha, the historic Buddha. Then we have the Sambhogakaya Buddha, another form of the Buddha, that is perceptible by and teaches only to Bodhisattvas on the higher bhumis. Finally, we have the Dharmakaya Buddha, the wisdom aspect of the Buddha, which is unoriginated and beyond form. So, we're taking refuge in the three kayas of the Buddha.

Taking Refuge in the Dharma

The second source of refuge is the Dharma. Going for refuge to the Dharma in an outer way means taking the Dharma as your path. You recognize that the way you can attain the state of Buddhahood, the way to follow the example of the Buddha, is to practice the Dharma that was taught by the Buddha.

When you go for refuge to the Dharma in an outer way, you are going for refuge to the path and its methods by which one frees oneself from mental affliction. This is called Satdharma, or genuine Dharma.

Dharma as symbol traditionally consists of books, letters, speech and thought. We have the Buddhist Canon. Then we have all kinds of other expressions of the speech aspect of Dharma, such as audio-dharma, video-dharma, hard copy dharma, CD Rom dharma, and one last thing: floppy dharma.

Trusting Satdharma as a path means trusting that the practice of

Dharma will increase your compassion. The practice of Dharma is a method that is necessary for us to use on our path to enlightenment. It is like a toolbox for liberation. In order to fix something like a screw, whether we have to loosen the screw or tighten the screw, we need a screwdriver. In a similar way we need the Dharma, we need the teachings of the Buddha in order to work with our problems; to find solutions for them and to fix them.

Traditionally, the Dharma is said to be like a boat. If you want to cross a lake or an ocean, you have to rely on a boat. Dharma is like the boat that helps you across. It helps you travel faster and not sink in this ocean of samsara.

So Dharma is the path. It is the words and wisdom of Buddha. It is simply one's own understanding, experience, and realization.

Our relationship with the Dharma is like our relationship with a boat. After we have crossed the water, there's no need for us to carry the boat. Therefore, after we have crossed the ocean of samsara, we no longer take external refuge in the Dharma. At that point, we have realized the nature of and are inseparable from Dharma. We have become Dharma. That is the second refuge in the outer sense.

Taking Refuge in the Sangha

The third source of refuge is the Sangha. The Sangha is the community of noble realized beings. This refuge also has the same external symbolic aspect. The external aspect of the Sangha to which one goes for refuge is first and foremost the retinue of Lord Buddha endowed with wisdom.

From the Mahayana point of view, this refers to Bodhisattvas like Arya Manjushri, Avalokiteshvara and so forth. From the Hinayana point of view, it refers to the great arhats such as Mahakashyapa, Ananda, and Shariputra. The Sangha of ordinary individuals refers to all of those who have transmitted the Dharma, the teachings of Buddha, as an unbroken succession or lineage up to the present day through their wisdom and compassion. We take refuge in the noble Sangha as our companion on the path.

Without the help of the Sangha, there's no way we can really enter the path. Historically, they are the people who received teachings from the Buddha. They then collected all of these teachings and put them on paper. Without the noble Sangha, we would not have any of these words, we would not have any literature of Dharma.

We take refuge in the Sangha as our companion because without them we wouldn't have the physical presence of the Dharma. Without them, we wouldn't have the genuine lineage of the Dharma, the realization of the Dharma, or the path of the Dharma. From the time of the noble Sangha up until now, the time of our present great masters, we have the continuity of the teachings, the continuity of the enlightened path.

PROVISIONAL AND ULTIMATE REFUGE

The Dharma and Sangha, the second and third sources of refuge, are considered to be provisional or temporary sources of refuge in the sense that once the path is completed you no longer need them. You have become the Buddha. The Buddha is considered to be an ultimate source of refuge in that you are continually sustained by or protected by your own Buddha Nature, which is the substance of your awakening as well.

In the traditional simile of the Dharma as boat, our personal teacher is the captain of the boat and embodies the companionship of the Sangha. When we take refuge in the Dharma and Sangha in this way, we rely to a certain degree on their help until we are across the lake or the ocean. When we're trying to get from one side of the water to the other side, we need the boat and the boatman to row us across. But once we get to the other side, we don't need the boatman any more because we are already there.

Right now we're on this side of the lake, not the other side, so we still need them. Once we are across the lake, it is logical that we don't have to carry the boat around. After we reach a certain point, we have to learn how to walk on our own feet, leaving the boat and captain behind. We just leave the boat behind, we just leave the captain. We don't bother him so much.

Therefore, taking refuge in Dharma and Sangha is not really the ultimate refuge. The ultimate refuge is the Buddha, the wisdom of the Buddha. We temporarily take refuge in the Dharma and Sangha, which is like going for help to the ship and the ship's captain.

That is our symbolic refuge in the refuge ceremony. We are taking refuge in the external, historic Buddha; his teachings, the Dharma; and the Sangha as our companion.

INNER REFUGE

The innermost sense of refuge is the discovery of our own basic nature of mind, which is the nature of Buddha's wisdom. The nature of Buddhahood itself is luminous, naturally cognizant wisdom. It is usually referred to as the Dharmakaya, or the body of essential qualities.

Inner Refuge in the Buddha

In the context of absolute truth, we go for refuge to the fundamental nature of our own mind, which is indivisible from the jewel of the Buddha. Our fundamental state of mind is totally awake, totally in the state of fully awakened heart. That's what Buddha is.

Rediscovering that heart, making a connection with that heart again, is what we call taking refuge in the Buddha. Buddha is basically the wisdom of awakened mind; which is nothing outside. It is within the very nature of our mind. Making a strong connection with that discovery is what we call taking refuge. It is an extremely, extremely close connection. That connection is basic confidence, basic faith. It is the basic trust that we develop through our discovery.

We're making a commitment to discover our own basic nature as being the wisdom of Buddha and to uncover it. We are making a commitment to work on developing our basic potential of Buddha, the Dharmakaya Buddha. Dharmakaya is always within our being, within all sentient beings.

On the one hand, we possess the basic qualities of the Buddha from beginningless time: We are Buddha from beginningless time. On the other hand, this Buddha quality potential is covered by our defilements and our obscurations.

The klesha mind and cognitive obscurations are covering our basic Buddha qualities. So we make a commitment that we are going to work on clearing these obstacles and generating our basic Buddha quality to the extent that we can fully radiate this quality outside as a Buddha. That is the fundamental notion of taking refuge in the Buddha as being within our own nature.

To recognize that the nature of our mind is Buddha Nature is the beginning of the process of revealing that nature. By revealing that nature, we can dispel all the sufferings and all of the fears of samsara. To recognize that our mind's nature is Buddha Nature, to have confidence or faith in this, and to have the aspiration and commitment to reveal it, is the internal way of going for refuge.

Inner Refuge in the Dharma

Taking refuge in the Dharma in the inner sense is becoming one with the path of fully developing this discovery of the essential nature of mind. At this point, whatever we have discovered as an enlightened heart is not yet fully grown. It is not yet at the stage of full grown enlightened mind.

Our discovery is still a little shaky. It is a very, very profound discovery but at the same time it's very shaky and very tricky. At a certain point, it becomes very clear, and we're very confident.

On the other hand, we have lots of doubts. We have lots of shaky states that we go through which means we have not fully developed this discovery. We have not fully mastered or familiarized ourselves with the new discovery or reconnection that we have made. Therefore, we are taking refuge in the Dharma that is the genuine path.

That genuine path is nothing but your realization on the path. It is the internalization of Dharma, making yourself one with the Dharma instead of looking at Dharma as a path that is outside you. That is the innermost sense of taking refuge in the Dharma. It is becoming one with the path, becoming one with the teachings. It is going beyond the language and words of Dharma and simply being Dharma. Being in the state of Dharma, being in the state of path, is what we call taking refuge in Dharma. Taking refuge in Dharma involves a complete trust, a complete confidence, and a complete sense of being which is the mindfulness of mind.

The Ultimate Dharma, the refuge of Dharma connected with absolute truth, is the arisal of Dharma in your mind. It is the mixing of the meaning of Dharma with your mind such that your actions and states of body, speech and mind are always in accordance with the Dharma. It is the point at which your mind and the Dharma are totally mixed, and you become the Dharma.

So the real Dharma is realization. As an ultimate source of refuge, it is not anything outside you or separate from your mind. Nevertheless, in order to increase one's realization of ultimate Dharma, one goes for refuge to the Dharma, which is the commitment to generating and increasing this realization.

Although Buddha Nature is

present within you, it is not revealed. It is still hidden or obscured. Its presence and the recognition of, or trust in, its presence are not in themselves enough to dispel the sufferings of samsara. In order to actually dispel those sufferings, you have to fully reveal this Buddha Nature. You have to make its qualities manifest. The process of revealing it involves enhancing or developing both wisdom and compassion. The methods by which it can be revealed are what we call Dharma. To train in these profound methods for gradually revealing your own Buddha Nature is going for refuge in the genuine Dharma.

Inner Refuge in the Sangha

The third refuge is taking refuge in the Sangha. Taking refuge in the Sangha is the outcome of the first two. After you have discovered this

basic heart of enlightenment, after
you have familiarized yourself with
that and internalized it as the path,
then whatever result comes out of it
is what we call the Sangha. What
manifests from these first two
discoveries of enlightened heart and
the path of enlightenment is a
complete sense of compassionate
heart. The warmth, the loving heart
that manifests out of these
discoveries, is what we call taking
refuge in the Sangha.

So that is our companion. Our
companion is loving-kindness; our
companion is bodhicitta; our
companion is love for others; our
companion is compassion for others.
That is the notion of Sangha here and
of taking refuge in the Sangha in the
innermost sense. That is the true
refuge that we are taking. There is no
form involved. It is a simple,
genuine, straightforward heart that
you have discovered. Rediscovering

and strengthening that heart is what we call taking refuge.

When we become one with the Dharma and are in the process of generating this basic Buddha quality, then we are a part of the Sangha. The actual refuge of the Sangha arises when we realize the qualities of the truth of cessation and are then able to help and instruct others. The ultimate Sangha is what happens to our mind when we enter and progress on the path of Dharma. It happens when Dharma starts to become actualized within us. Through engaging in this process of revealing our own fundamental nature, our compassion for other beings as well as our natural wisdom increases and flourishes. As a result, we become able to benefit both ourselves and others.

This activity of benefiting ourselves and others is what is meant by going for refuge to the Sangha.

COMMITMENTS OF RESTRICTION

There are certain commitments associated with going for refuge. Having gone for refuge to the Buddha, it is taught that you should not seek the protection of or go for refuge to powerful, mundane beings, worldly deities, or lokapalas. The reason for this is that the ultimate refuge is your own innate Buddha Nature. No source of protection, no source of refuge, can match that. You have all of the necessary qualities complete within yourself.

It is unnecessary to try to acquire these from beings external to yourself. The image that is used for this is of someone who owns a vast treasury filled with jewels. It is unnecessary for such a person to go out and try to find jewels. In recognition of this, there's no need to go for refuge to mundane beings.

Having gone for refuge to the Dharma, it is taught that you should abandon all that is harmful to other beings. At best, one should actively help. Failing that, one should try to refrain from engaging in any attitude or action that would produce pain in others. Even in situations where you cannot benefit other beings, you should do your best to minimize, as much as possible, whatever harm you do to them.

Having gone for refuge to the Sangha, it is taught that when you find yourself in situations where your friends, your companions, or your entire environment are leading you away from the Dharma, you should exercise mindfulness and vigilance. If you let go of your mindfulness and vigilance in such a situation, you will become unable to help others. Further, you will be at risk of being led astray. So long as one has no ability to actually help others, then one is more likely to be influenced by others than to influence them.

If you constantly accompany people who actively destroy your virtuous tendencies, then not only will your virtue be easily destroyed but they will also further destroy their own. The situation will harm everyone involved.

We can use the example of people who are involved in negative karmas like hunting, fishing, and so forth. If we hang around with these friends too much at the beginning stage of our practice of Dharma, we might become influenced by them. We might start thinking, "Well, maybe it's interesting. Maybe it's nice to fish or shoot." Something like that may occur in our minds. We may decide to try it once or twice. Then we get drawn into the situation and get involved in negative karma.

But once our practice has been strengthened, then it is important for us to be there and try to help in whatever way we can.

Our commitment is to be more mindful and aware when we go out into our regular samsaric world. The world that we live in has a lot of sharp edges. If we are not mindful and aware, we may get cut by these sharp edges instead of turning them into beautiful flowers. Until we actually generate the qualities associated with the path, our commitment is to exercise some caution in allowing ourselves to come under the influence of people or groups who are actively engaged in things that harm others.

So these three are called the Commitments of Restriction.

COMMITMENTS OF PERFORMANCE

There are three supplementary commitments, which are known as the Commitments of Performance. They're quite simple. They are to respect, especially in your attitude, the symbols of the Buddha, Dharma and Sangha. After taking refuge in the Buddha, we respect all forms of the Buddha, such as statues, pictures, paintings or any images of the Buddha. It is the same for the Dharma and the Sangha. We show respect for the texts and for symbols of the communities of ordained men and women. For example, we should not walk over a statue of the Buddha or a text that we have left on our cushion.

It is important to understand that respect here does not mean adopting any particular cultural form. The point is the internal attitude of respect, not particularly how it is demonstrated externally. So this is not an injunction to attempt to adopt a particular cultural form. You should demonstrate respect with body, speech and mind in a way that is in accordance with your cultural background.

DEDICATIONS OF MERIT

By whatever boundless merit we
    have attained
Through hearing this precious,
    genuine dharma of the supreme
    yana
May all beings become a stainless
    vessel
Of the precious, genuine dharma of
    the supreme yana.

This was written by Asanga.

By this virtue, may all beings
Perfect the accumulations of merit
    and wisdom
And achieve the two genuine kayas
Arising from merit and wisdom.

This was written by Nagarjuna.

POEM

Paint it no more

True reflection

Let it Float

In the True Light of Space

The Dzogchen Ponlop Rinpoche
Karme Choling, 1996

BIOGRAPHICAL INFORMATION

Dzogchen Ponlop Rinpoche

Dzogchen Ponlop Rinpoche, acknowledged as one of the foremost scholars and educators of his generation in the Nyingma and Kagyu schools of Tibetan Buddhism, was born at Rumtek Monastery (Dharma Chakra Center) in Sikkim, India in 1965, where he was recognized by His Holiness the 16th Gyalwang Karmapa and enthroned in 1968.

Rinpoche received Buddhist refuge and bodhisattva vows from His Holiness Karmapa at an early age. He received the complete teachings and empowerments of the Kagyu and Nyingma traditions from His Holiness Karmapa, His Holiness Dilgo Khyentsé, Rinpoche, Khenpo Tsultrim Gyamtso Rinpoche and others. In May, 1990, Rinpoche graduated from the Karma Shri Nalanda Institute for

Higher Buddhist Studies as an Acharya, or Master of Buddhist Philosophy. He also studied comparative religions at Columbia University in New York City.

Rinpoche is fluent in the English language and is an accomplished calligrapher, visual artist and poet. Known for his sharp intellect, humor, and the lucidity of his teaching, Rinpoche uses his deep understanding of both Eastern and Western cultures to teach throughout the world.

Nitartha *international*

In 1994, to assist in the integration of computer technology with traditional Tibetan scholarship, Rinpoche founded Nitartha *international*, a non-profit education corporation based in New York City. Nitartha uses computer technologies to support Tibetan studies and education, and preserves the ancient literature of Tibet in computerized formats.

In addition to his work in traditional Tibetan educational institutions, Rinpoche works actively to develop and adapt traditional Tibetan education curriculums for Western audiences. In 1995 he helped establish Nitartha Institute in North America, which provides a focused Tibetan studies program for Westerners.

Nalandabodhi

In 1997, Rinpoche founded Nalandabodhi, an association of Buddhist meditation and study centers to preserve the genuine lineage of the Nyingma and Kagyu Schools of Tibetan Buddhism. The spiritual head of Nalandabodhi is Rinpoche's main teacher, Khenpo Tsultrim Gyamtso Rinpoche.

In 1998, at the request of His Holiness, the Seventeenth Gyalwa Karmapa, Rinpoche became director of the Kamalashila Institute, the primary Kagyu educational and practice center in Germany. Rinpoche is also a regular visiting professor at Naropa University in Boulder, Colorado.

Additional information on the
activities of
Dzogchen Ponlop Rinpoche
can be found at
www.nalandabodhi.org
and
www.nitartha.org.

In Canada, please contact:
Nalandabodhi Foundation
Post Office Box 2355
Vancouver, British Columbia
Canada V6B 3W5

In the United States, please contact:
Nalandabodhi
5501 Seventeenth Avenue, N.E.
Seattle, Washington 98105

Nitartha *international*
1914 Bigelow Avenue North
Suite 5
Seattle, Washingon 98109

BOOKS FROM
SIDDHI PUBLICATIONS

Profound View, Fearless Path
The Bodhisattva Vow
Dzogchen Ponlop, Rinpoche

Turning Towards Liberation
Dzogchen Ponlop, Rinpoche

The Essence of Benefit and Joy:
A Method for the Saving of Lives
Jamgon Kongtrul Lodro Thaye